C000092676

Adelheid Dang

TATTED
BUTTERFLIES

Akacia

Drawings: Kirstine Nikolajsen and Inge Lise Nikolajsen

Forlaget Akacia
Skovvænget 1
DK - 5690 Tommerup
akacia@akacia.dk

© All rights reserved. No part of this book may be reproduced in any form, by print, photoprint, microfilm, microfiche, mechanical recording, photocopying, translation, or by any means, known or as yet unknown, or stored in any information retrieval system without written permission being obtained beforehand from the publishers.

Printed at Øko-Tryk I/S, Videbæk, Denmark, 2002

ISBN: 87-7847-054-4

INTRODUCTION

I love butterflies and for many years tatted butterflies have been one of my favourites.

This beautiful, little insect is perfect for tatting and for this booklet I have made twenty designs.

The butterflies are of different size and they use many different tatting tecniques – some are for beginners while others need some experience.

Use them for decorations on cards, on boxes, on pillows, on your clothes, on hankerchiefs and doilies, let them fly in your window or let them stay on your curtain – the possibilities are innumerable.

I hope, it will give you just as much pleasure making the butterflies as it gave me designing them.

Happy tatting.

Adelheid Dangela

EXPLANATION OF SYMBOLS

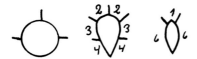 = Picots for joining or ornamentation. The figures are the number of double stitches

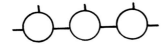 = Joining of picots in the same round

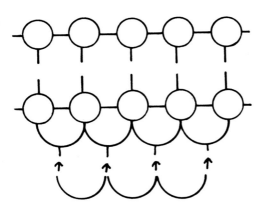 = Joining of rounds (picots pointing at each other)

= The arrows mark where to join the chains

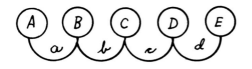 = A B C D E succession of rings. *a b c d e* succession of chains

= Josephine knot

 = Split ring
The side of the ring which is marked is tatted with lock stitches.

 = Alternately a normal stitch and a lock stitch.

 = Long picot with a knot to gather the threads.

= Long picot twisted twice.

ALFA

1 shuttle
The butterfly is made of 4 rings
- commence with ring A.

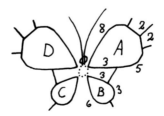

BIRTE

2 shuttles
The butterfly is made
continously - commence at
ring A.
The antennae are made of a
long picot which has been cut.

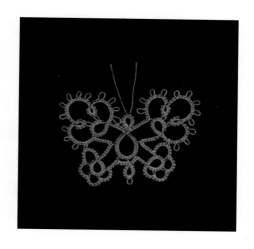

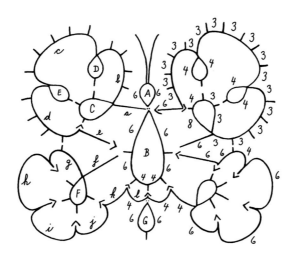

CELINE

2 shuttles
The butterfly is made
continously - commence
at ring A.

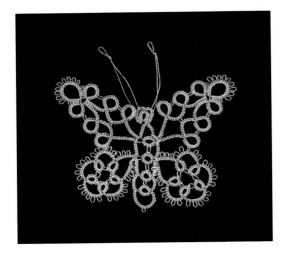

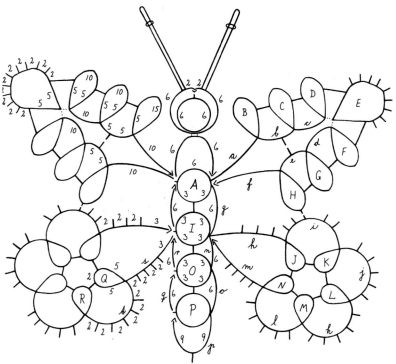

DIANA

2 shuttles
The body of the butterfly and one of the wings are made continuously.
Commence at ring A and tat the body with chain upon chain.
Continue with chain a at the wing without breaking the thread.
Tat the other wing and join it to the body.

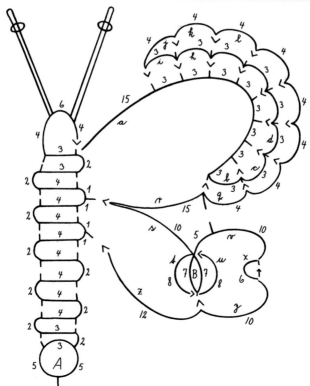

ELISE

2 shuttles
The right wing and the body
are made continously - commence at ring A. The left wing is
tatted separately and joined to the
body.

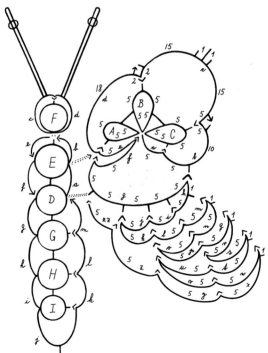

FLORA

2 shuttles
First tat the body - commence at
ring A.
Tat the wings separately -
follow the diagrams carefully.

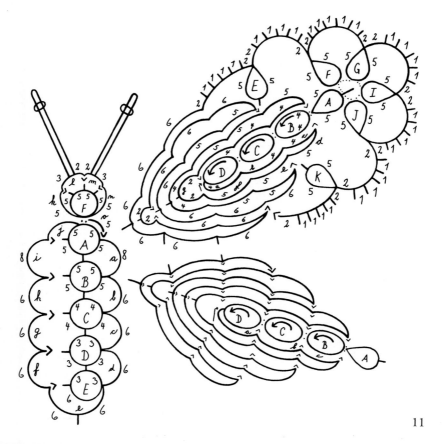

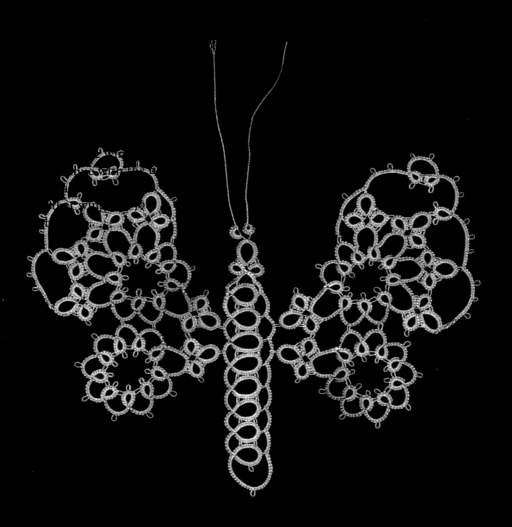

IRIS

IRIS

2 shuttles
The body and the wings are
made separately.

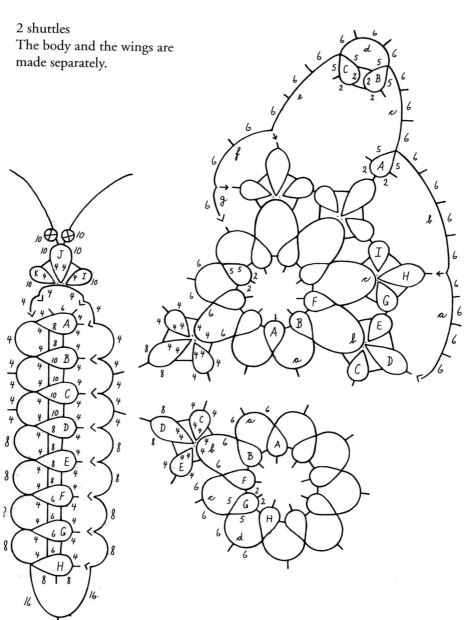

JOSIE

JOSIE

1 shuttle + a ball thread
Tat the upper and lower part of the wing separately and join them with the outer round.
Tat the body separately - commence at ring A and continue with chains.
Make the antennae last.

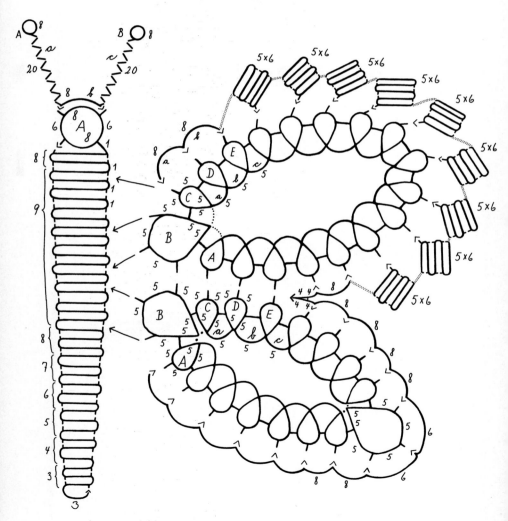

KIRSTEN

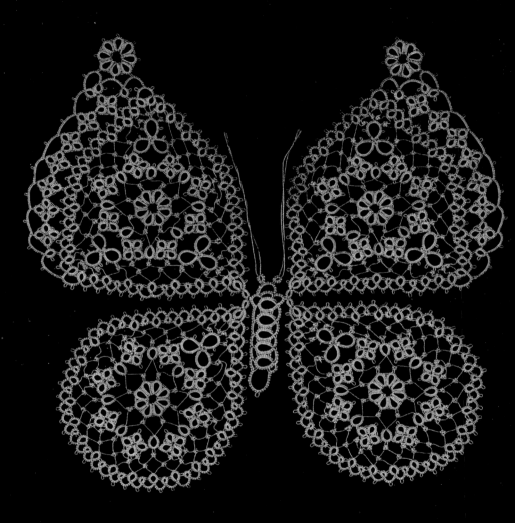

KIRSTEN

1 shuttle + a ball thread
The different parts of the butterfly are made separately.
First tat the body - commence at ring A. Add the head - commence at ring a.
The antennae are long, cut picots.

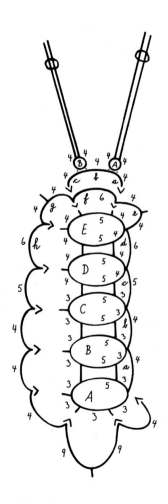

KIRSTEN - continued

The lower part of the wing.
Commence at the flower in the middle.
The threfoil and the four-leaf clovers are tatted one by one.
Join the wing to the body as shown on the picture.

KIRSTEN - continued

The upper part of the wing:
The wing is made according to the diagram and joined to the body in the
same picot as the lower part of the wing - see picture.

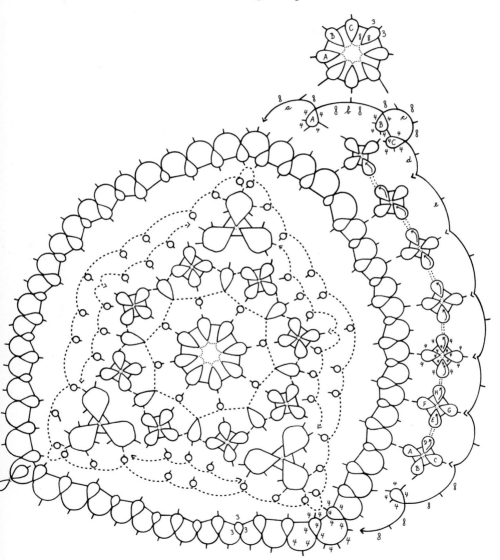

LINDA

2 shuttles
First make the upper part of
the wing.
Tat the body separately.

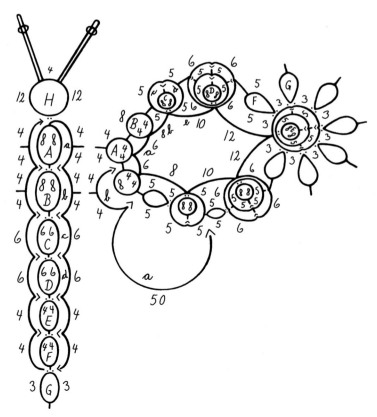

GRETE

2 shuttles

First make the wing - commence at cluny leaf A. Continue with cluny leaf B and then chain a. Then the cluny leaves are joined in the middle to make a flower.

When the wing is finished continue with the body without breaking the thread.

Tat the left wing separately and join it to the body.

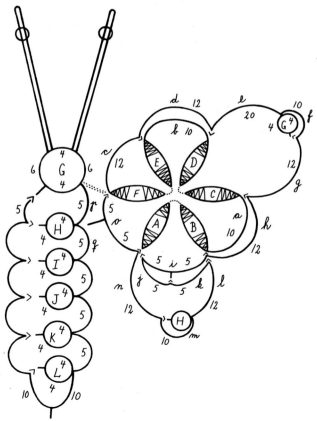

NORA

2 shuttles
Make the upper and lower part of the wing one by one and join them with the outer round. The body is tatted separately and joined at the wings.

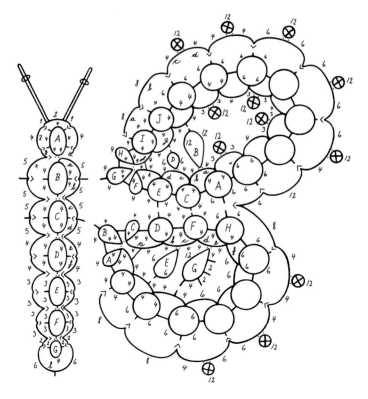

TERESA

2 shuttles
Make the butterfly in one round -
commence at ring A.
Please observe that the long picots
in the wings are twisted.

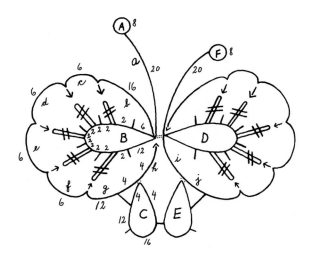

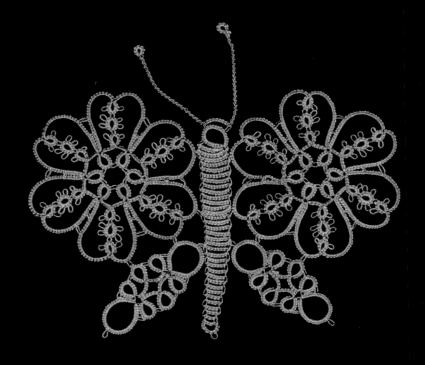

OLIVIA

2 shuttles

The upper part of the wing is made in 2 rounds. The rings b - B are tatted as chain b and ring B (ring upon ring).

The lower part of the wing is tatted continously.

The body is tatted separately - commence at ring A and continue with chain upon chain.

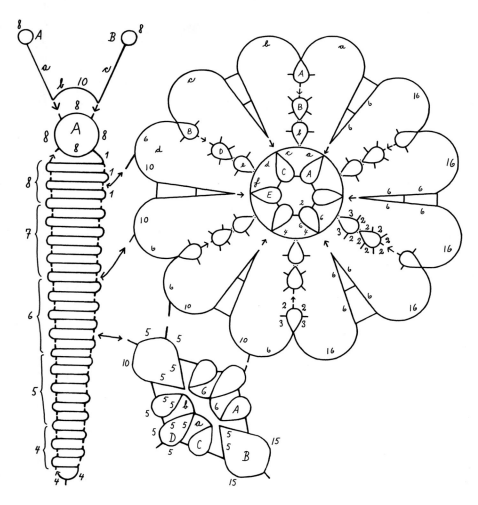

PAULA

2 shuttles.
Make the wings chain upon
chain.
At last tat the body and join
it to the wings.

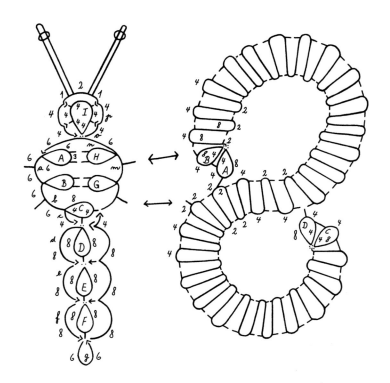

RICARDA

2 shuttles
Ricarda evolved from Paula.
The wings are made chain on
chain.
At last make the body and join
it to the wings.

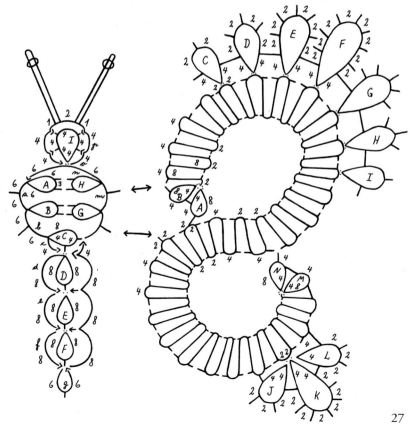

SIBYLLE

SIBYLLE

2 shuttles.
Make the wing in two rounds. There is ring upon ring in both rounds.
Tat the body separately.

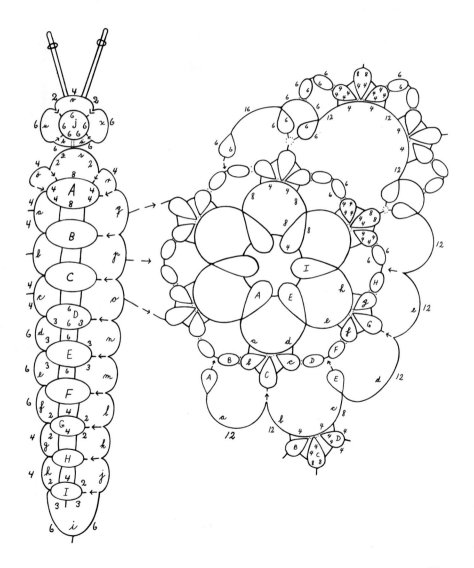

VIOLA

2 shuttles.
Make each part separately.

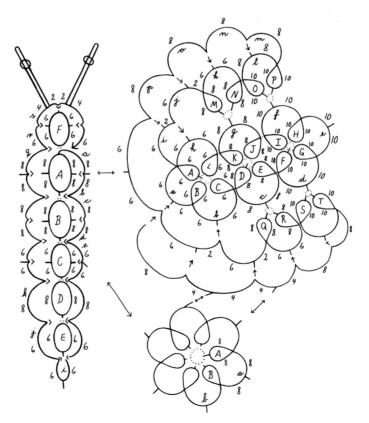

MIA

1 shuttle + a ball thread.
First make the body.
Tat the wings separately and
join them to the body.

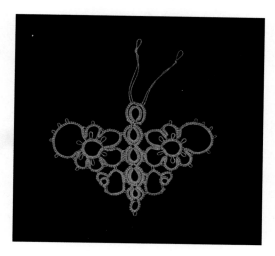

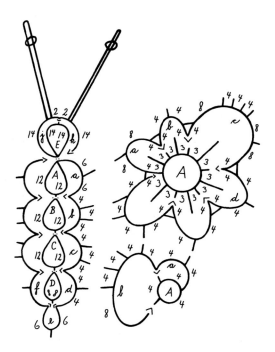

The butterfly can be placed at the corner of a handkerchief or as shown here around an octagonal doily.